SCRIPOPHILY
HISTORIC BOND & SHARE COLLECTING

Ian Moncrief-Scott

Information Management Solutions Limited

ISLE OF MAN

The author Ian Moncrief-Scott has asserted his right under the Copyright, Designs and Patents Act 1988 to be identified as the author of this work.

Copyright. © I. Moncrief-Scott 2021

All rights reserved. No part of this publication may be produced in any form or by any means - graphic, electronic, or mechanical, including photocopying, recording, taping, or information storage and retrieval systems - without the prior permission in writing of the publishers.

The publishers make no representation, express or implied, regarding the accuracy of the information contained in this book and cannot accept any legal responsibility for any errors or omissions that may take place.

A CIP catalogue record for this book is available from the British Library.

Published by Information Management Solutions Limited, 17 Howe Road, Onchan, Isle of Man, IM3 2BB.

Printed, bound and distributed by IngramSpark.

Book Layout © 2017 BookDesignTemplates.com

Superhero Peg Image: Besjunior/Shutterstock.com

Cover Source by Tanja Prokop of BookDesignTemplates.com

SCRIPOPHILY: HISTORIC BOND & SHARE COLLECTING – 2nd ed.
ISBN 9781903467084

The Publishers have been requested by the author to acknowledge the direct and indirect contributions to this book by:

American Museum of Finance
Bank of England Museum
De La Rue PLC
Financial Services Authority
International Bond & Share Society
The Rothschild Archive

This book is dedicated to
start-up entrepreneurs.

The front cover depicts
ordinary wooden clothes pegs dressed as
Super Heroes.

**All start-up entrepreneurs are
ordinary people
turning into Super Heroes!**

CONTENTS

SCRIPOPHILY 1
OTHER BOOKS BY THE AUTHOR 11
FORTHCOMING BOOKS BY THE AUTHOR 13

SCRIPOPHILY

Imagine, you could acquire millions of pounds in international investments for relatively nothing!

A pyramid scam? The dubious sale of a national monument? No, Scripophily.

Old share and bond collecting is arguably the world's fastest-growing hobby and investment opportunity. Attracting 120,000 collectors in twenty years, denounced financial documents are seeing a valuable renaissance.

Henry Wells and William Fargo could not have possibly conceived that routine American Express papers, signed 150 years ago, would today realise over £1000 each.

Scripophily has ensured that.

In 1978, the blossoming hobby needed a name. The Times ran a competition. Scrip, short for subscription receipt, a debt acknowledgement loosely meaning shares, was fused with Philos, Greek for loving.

The love of shares was born.

Enthusiasts have their own favourite subjects. Some relish ornate illustrations and artistic content. Others appreciate the explosive development of commerce, roads, railways, bridges, canals, banking dynasties, shipping lines, states and nations.

Certificates range from postcard to opened broadsheet newspaper size, which many collectors proudly display on the walls of their homes and offices. Securities make good taking points and unusual gifts for friends, colleagues and clients.

Scripophilists argue that shares and bonds have greater historical significance than paintings, stamps or banknotes. Per square inch, they offer better value for money.

Sometimes, the attraction is a signature, made famous by the passage of time. A Standard oil founder's share, signed by John D Rockefeller, can change hands for over $60,000.

Russian loan certificates, though generally in poor condition, but hand-signed by Nathan Mayer Rothschild in 1822, will fetch £70-£100. The forerunner to Getty Oil, Mission Development Company bearing John Paul Getty's autograph, can be yours for under £10.

Modern shares are not entirely ignored. Redundant copies of Walt Disney or Planet Hollywood stock with the facsimile signatures of Stallone, Arnie, and Willis already fetch £65.

However, history fascinates many. Railroad companies that interlaced the frontier towns of America, funded by $1000 certificates redeemable in gold coin, Britain's Stockton & Darlington Railway Company, The Confederacy.

Other collectors favour themes, insurance, hotels, animals, cars, aircraft, mining, or entertainment. The list is endless. Some choose countries like Brazil, Costa Rica, Mexico, Egypt, Romania, China, and Russia.

Major international bond launches were printed in Great Britain.

Bradbury Wilkinson & Co Limited and Waterlow & Sons Limited, now part of the De La Rue Group, which prints UK banknotes, and remains the globe's premier securities' producer, were selected for these large, colourful and intricate products.

Though the vast majority of certificates are discharged or reneged, some could yet be fulfilled. China and Russia are still at the forefront of defaulted national debt.

Owners remain hopeful that eventually their trust will be repaid.

Only a decade ago, with the help of the Bank of England, UK holders of eighty-year-old defunct Russian debt received partial payments.

Researching a bond or share increases interest and adds value when you come to sell. Bonds can relate intrigue, power-lust, spectacular collapse, fraud, and even murder. They reflect the aspirations and, in some cases, the miserable failure of enterprises and governments.

Documents usually have a story to tell. Canada is a rich source of the world's precious minerals, the Klondike Gold Rush, immortalised by Charlie Chaplin, an early instance.

Harsh weather and topography caused many failures. Fred Stark Pearson, director of the San Antonio Land and Irrigation Company Limited and his associate Alfred Lowenstein, who also built electric tramways in Brazil, Mexico and Spain, were famous entrepreneurs of the time.

Pearson drowned in 1915 when a German submarine torpedoed the Lusitania.

Mysteriously, Lowenstein fell from his own aircraft when travelling to France in 1928. Krueger & Toll, a Swedish company, which once dominated the world's match business, was finished by rumours of fraud.

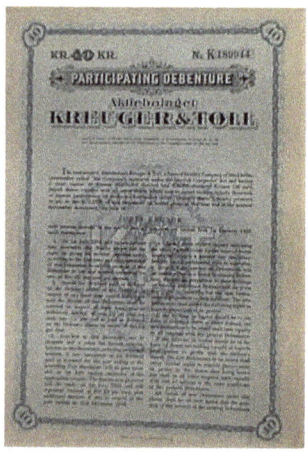

Where do you find them? Phillips and Christies now hold three specific auctions a year. International dealers will offer you comprehensive illustrated catalogues and webpages.

Thirty international auction houses prove the rising trend. Regular monthly postal and live auctions take place in Germany, the USA, Switzerland, and Belgium.

The UK has a dedicated promotion group, the International Bond & Share Society, founded in 1978, which issues a quarterly magazine with a free bulletin board and an annual directory of members.

Corresponding clubs and societies encourage collectors in Europe, Australia, South Africa, the USA and Canada. Occasionally, a valuable bond is unearthed when sorting a deceased relative's cupboards. Junk shops, curio arcades, car-boot sales, and deed boxes all reveal interesting finds.

Now that the borders of China and Russia are open, caches should emerge. Meanwhile, the German government has a large stockpile, which it is considering releasing to the public.

As companies rely on computerised records, original historical chronicles will increase in rarity, and ultimately, in value. Unfortunately, recent EU data-protection legislation could hasten the destruction of irreplaceable investment paperwork.

Remember, shares and certificates were working documents, made to be handled. They can show serious signs of wear. But beware, the ravages of time may not necessarily detract from a share's worth, if only poor samples are known to exist.

Always try to obtain the best example.

Formal classification has evolved from the banknote and stamp fields. Mint, uncirculated, very fine, cancelled are all identifiable terms, but rarity and popularity have an overriding influence.

Despite huge public offerings, many Russian certificates are rare because of their turbulent history. However, not many people collect them, so they are inexpensive.

On the other hand, American railroad shares are hugely popular internationally and can command a disproportionate price.

Storing certificates carefully is essential. Many have been folded for storage in the past and you must take care when preserving them. The folds, while being a weak point, add to the character and opening them out should reduce further deterioration. Try to keep your collection flat in a dry secure place.

Mice, spiders and mould can play havoc with prices! Protective acid-free tissue covers are best. Artists' satchels can be useful for storage and transport.

If you decide to display your prized possessions, make sure that your framer uses acid-free and UV stabilized glass. Never hang your showpiece in direct sunlight, it will fade.

A good practise when building your collection is to record the source, price and any identifying marks. Colour copies of a valuable piece can be a wise investment. Make sure that your domestic insurance covers your collection, particularly when you buy expensive items.

Your Scripophily collection can be acquired modestly, swapping and selling unwanted items as you develop a particular area of interest. It will increase in value, but experts would advise buying what you enjoy, rather than for investment.

Next time you visit that old aunt or uncle, ask if they have any redundant shares, you might make their retirement even happier.

OTHER BOOKS BY THE AUTHOR

As Good As Gold - History of Pound Sterling. ISBN 0-9534818-4-0

De La Rue Straw Hats to Global Securities. ISBN 0- 9534818-2-4

Euro History & Development. ISBN 0-9534818-1-6

Holidays 2000 – A Time Capsule. ISBN 0-9534818-7-5

Negotiate to Win! - The Introductory Edition. ISBN 0-9534818-6-7

Start Any Business (Print). ISBN 9781903467008
Start Any Business (eBook). ISBN 9781903467015

Scripophily - Historic Bond & Share Collecting. ISBN 0-9534818-5-9
Scripophily (eBook). ISBN 9781903467176

The Eternal Old Lady - Bank of England. ISBN 0-9534818-3-2

The Green Shoots of Money (Print). ISBN 9781903467107
The Green Shoots of Money (eBook). ISBN 9781903467114

The Hitmen - Part One. ISBN 0-9534818-8-3

FORTHCOMING BOOKS BY THE AUTHOR

As Good As Gold (Print). ISBN 9781903467039
As Good As Gold (eBook). ISBN 9781903467121

Currants, Olives & Cotton (Print). ISBN 9781903467077
Currants, Olives & Cotton (eBook). ISBN 9781903467169

De La Rue (Print). ISBN 9781903467046
De La Rue (eBook). ISBN 9781903467138

Euro (Print). ISBN 9781903467053
Euro (eBook). ISBN 9781903467145

Tail-less Cats & Three-legged Men (Print). ISBN 9781903467091
Tail-less Cats & Three-legged Men (eBook). ISBN 9781903467183

The Eternal Old Lady (Print). ISBN 9781903467060
The Eternal Old Lady (eBook). ISBN 9781903467152

ABOUT THE AUTHOR

Ian Moncrief-Scott has over fifty years of broad business experience, mostly gained at international level, based in the UK.

As a former senior executive for a global publishing and information technology company headquartered in the USA, he has contributed to numerous client-facing procurement and outsourcing initiatives worldwide.

Ian has created and participated in numerous small businesses in the UK, Isle of Man and elsewhere.

He has also represented the Isle of Man Government Department for Enterprise in several of its business support schemes. Ian designed and delivered extensive training for its Micro Business Grant Scheme.

In recognition of his long-term service to the Department, Ian was nominated for The Queen's Award for Enterprise Promotion and awarded an official Certificate of Recognition in 2018.

Throughout his career, he has maintained an active interest in start-ups, especially those involving the financial sector.

At the turn of the millennium, several of the articles written by Ian that form this short work were originally published by the Museum of American Financial History (now the Museum of American Finance).

www.ingramcontent.com/pod-product-compliance
Lightning Source LLC
Chambersburg PA
CBHW042000080526
44588CB00021B/2823